Paint Your Own
NEON
Stones

h
hinkler

KATIE CAMERON

NEON PAINTED ROCKS

Rock art is one of the most ancient forms of artistic expression known to humans, and creating rock art has recently become a hugely popular pastime. Using neon paint is a fantastic way to add a brilliant glow to your rocky works of art, highlighting and adding a fun, eye-catching element. Brighten up your home or garden with some dazzling neon pieces or light up a friend's day with a gorgeous gift.

There are eight wonderful neon rock-painting activities in this book, including boldly simple designs, intricate geometric arrangements and cute character pieces. Many of the designs draw on the natural world, taking their inspiration from creatures of the sea and air, as well as from the stars.

You don't need to be a skilled painter to create these colourful artworks – anyone can do it! The act of creating neon painted rocks can be a fun and fulfilling way to spend a few hours. You can paint just about anything on a stone, transforming it from an everyday garden rock to a fantastic little piece of art. Take your art to the next step and really make your rocks stand out using vibrant neon paint!

CONTENTS

GETTING STARTED

YOU WILL NEED A FEW THINGS BEFORE YOU CAN GET STARTED ON YOUR ACTIVITIES.

STONES

The best stones to paint on are smooth and relatively free of cracks or holes. Stones that are too rough or pitted are not ideal because the paint will run and neat detailing is difficult to achieve. Rounded stones make for nice symmetry, although you can paint on stones of any shape. Keep in mind that the larger the stone, the longer it will generally take to complete.

If you are going to gather your own stones (rock hunting is often half the fun!), smooth stones are most often found along the shores of oceans and rivers. But if this is not an option or you want to save time, smooth stones can be purchased from craft stores.

IMPORTANT: *Make sure it is OK to take the stones from your area. Some places have regulations to protect the environment against things like erosion or risks to animal habitats, and sometimes it can also be culturally inappropriate. Ensure that you always ask permission if taking from private property.*

Be sure to thoroughly clean your stones. Rinse off the bulk of any mud or sand outside (not down the kitchen drain!), and then give them a scrub in the sink with soap and water. Ensure that the stones are free of any dust or debris and are completely dry before you begin.

WORK SPACE

You will need a large, well-lit work station with enough space for you to paint and also have everything you need within arm's reach. Your station should be high enough to maintain good posture, and be equipped with a comfortable chair. Painting these beautiful stones can take a lot of time, so be aware of the time you're spending and try not to sit for too long! Be sure to get up, stretch and move around for ten minutes or so at least once an hour. Movement is good for your body's circulation and can also help you refocus.

To keep your work space neat and tidy, place a piece of cardboard or paper towel beneath your stone before you begin, and protect the remainder of your space with old newspaper. The cardboard helps to keep the underside of the stone clean and can also be helpful if you wish to move the stone to another area without needing to pick it up.

HANDY HINT

Have the paint colours you plan to use, or have been using, set aside. This comes in handy if you are mixing a new shade, picking up where you left off, or if you are applying a second coat. You don't want to apply a second coat in the wrong colour!

PAINTS

Regular craft or student acrylic paint works well for painting stones. It is non-toxic, intermixable, fast drying and adheres well to a stone's surface. It's also cheap and easy to clean using a little soap and water. Most acrylic paint is easily intermixable. You can mix new colour combinations, darken shades with a little black or add white to lighten shades.

Be aware that neon acrylic colours are not alike across all brands. The intensity of the colour varies, as does the opacity. In general, neon colours are translucent. Regular acrylic paint is largely opaque, meaning it will apply in one or two coats without being see-through. Neon paints require several coats to appear intense in colour and so that you cannot see what is beneath.

To save time and paint, prime your rock using white paint or a bright acrylic paint of the same colour as your neon paint (for example, regular lime green paint as a base coat under neon green paint).

If you paint directly onto the stone, the dark surface of the stone will show through and the colour won't seem very neon. You can use this to your advantage: for instance, if you want a darker shade for the background or other detailing.

Allow neon paint to dry completely between coats or you may end up with streaks or uneven paint. Acrylic paint can take anywhere from 5–15 minutes to dry, depending on the thickness of the paint; though this is 'to the touch'. It can take 24 hours or more for acrylic craft paint to 'cure' to a point where it is completely dry and a maximum hardness.

Drying time is affected by many factors – how heavily it is applied, temperature, humidity, brand, colour and more. Don't touch the stone while it is drying; you risk leaving smudges or fingerprints. Even after the paint has dried, applying a finish can moisten it for a short time. The last thing you want at the final stage is a paint mishap, so hands off until you're sure the paint is firm!

HANDY HINT

Mix any colours you plan to use before you begin so you don't have to try to match the colour mix later. Mix more than you need, as it is often impossible to mix the exact shade again. Store any remaining paint for future use. Try neon pink and neon yellow for a bright peachy colour or neon blue and neon pink for a bright purple.

NOTES ABOUT NEON

Neon shades can be darkened with a little bit of black or lightened with a little white; however, you cannot make any new neon colours. Neon pigment is man-made and this brightness is generally limited to pink, orange, yellow, green, blue and red colours. You can intermix neon paint with regular acrylic paint to make some interesting new shades; the brightness will be muted but will still yield some fun colours. Just don't expect to make a new neon!

Regular colours absorb light while neon absorbs and re-emits it, causing it to appear bright. Fluorescent colours are made using chemicals that cause fluorescence, meaning they will glow under a black or UV light. Phosphorescence glows in the dark after you shine a light on it.

TOOLS

There are a few tools that are useful when painting rocks:

- Pencil and eraser – use these to sketch out your ideas and designs on paper beforehand. Light grey-lead pencil markings can be used directly on the stone or dry paint, and an eraser can remove any marks, or you can simply paint over them.

- Drawing compass and ruler – you can use your eye to judge measurements like centre points for designs and base coats, but a ruler and compass make this process much faster and easier. If symmetry is an important factor in your design, you will want precise and equal measurements on all sides. These tools are useful when forming new designs on paper. A compass may be difficult to use on some shapes of stones; if this is the case, use your judgement to visually choose the centre spot.

- Paintbrushes – pointed brushes are best for fine detailing and lines, dotting and touch-ups. Use a larger sized round or flat brush when painting areas that need more coverage (i.e. base coats). Generally, brushes with shorter handles and shorter, firmer bristles work better to achieve precise detailing. Dot formation will vary with the amount of paint on the brush and the pressure you use. For larger dots, use a brush with larger bristles. It is important to keep your brushes in good condition with the bristles straight and together. Never let brushes dry with paint on them, and only dip them into the paint to about half the hair length so the paint doesn't get on the ferrule (the little metal piece that attaches the bristles to brush handle). Getting paint on the ferrule will inevitably result in spreading and frayed bristles, no matter how much you wash your paintbrush. Have a little cup of water at your work station so that you can quickly wash off paint and keep brushes moist before washing them thoroughly with soap and water.

HANDY HINT

If you store a lot of paints in a drawer or container where you cannot see each label, brush a dab of paint on the top of the lid. This way you can easily see which colour is which, and how it will look when dry. When you only have a few small dots to do, save paint by dipping your stick in the paint left in the cap after you shake the container, rather than pouring it onto a palette. Just don't forget to put the cap back on!

- Paint or permanent-ink pens – these can be a little expensive but even just having black and white in an extra or ultra-fine tip can be invaluable. Use them to outline your design and to create extra-fine details that need to be all the same size, which can be very frustrating to achieve using paint and a brush!

- Dotting stylus – also known as a nail dotting tool or embosser, this looks similar to a pencil. It has a needle in one or both ends and a small round ball on the tip. This handy little device can be found at craft stores; it is fairly inexpensive and is fantastic for dotting in acrylic paint.

- Dotting tools – if you can't find a dotting stylus at your craft store, save money by using the pointed ends of household items. Think toothpicks, skewers, small dowels, unsharpened pencil ends, etc. These items allow greater precision and control when doing intricate dot work, and care is minimal as you do not have to clean them! You can allow the paint to dry on the sticks, which can layer and create new sizes for their ends; or you can pull off the dried paint and keep a small, pointed end.

HANDY HINT

If you're using dowels as dotting tools, you can sharpen them with a pencil sharpener or blade to create a variety of dotting sizes.

MAKING DOTS

To ensure accuracy when placing dots, hold the tool in one hand like a pencil and, if needed, steady the rock with the other hand. Try to hold the stick perpendicular to the stone, applying dots at a 90-degree angle. Steady your aim by resting your hand, wrist or elbow against the desk or the stone itself.

Increasing the size of each dot from one row to the next is mostly a matter of having the right amount of paint on the right-sized tool. Usually, the smaller the point, the smaller the dot; you can use the small pointed end of a toothpick or the very tip of the longest bristle in a round paintbrush for your smallest dots.

The smallest dots do not require a lot of paint to make a well-formed circular dot. Too much paint and you could place a dot too large. You will need to wipe clean and re-dip the tool into the paint after each dot and use the same amount of pressure to maintain saturation and equal dot sizing.

When you want to go up a dot size, you can use the same sized dotting tool with slightly more paint and add just a bit more pressure while touching the stick to stone. If you do not wipe the paint from the stick before re-dipping, it will start to dry and accumulate, enlarging the end of the tool. A bigger tool end will give a bigger size dot.

To increase dot size, you can also use a larger tool. The diameter of the end of the tool you are using is a good indication of the size of the dot it will create and, of course, the more it is saturated with paint, the bigger the dot will be.

CLEAR FINISH

Most craft stores stock affordable clear, gloss or matte acrylic finishes that will make your colours appear brighter and seal them in place longer. It will also protect against fading, and make your stones resistant to water and weather conditions. The spray-on type is preferable to the brush-on type, as this is quick and easy, and adheres to all parts of the stone in a uniform, even manner.

Always wait until your stone is complete, the paint is completely dry and hard, and the stone is free of any dust or unwanted particles before spraying the protective finish in a well-ventilated room or outside. Allow at least a day for the finish to dry, then apply a second coat and allow it to dry again. As with paint, avoid touching your stone while the finish is drying to ensure the coating hardens smoothly.

If you do not wish to use a protective finish, try using acrylic 'outdoor' paints, which are designed with a finish built in. These outdoor craft paints are more durable than regular acrylic paints; however, they cost more, and are not as durable as a separate finishing coat.

Some paint or permanent-ink pens can bleed or smear when finish is applied. If you are using these pens, make sure you test how they react to a finish *before* you apply the finish to your stone. To do this, use your pen on some dry white paint on the underside of a stone. Ensure the paint is dry before applying a clear finish to see the result. If the ink reacts with the finish, it will blur into the white paint. You might want to either skip the finish or apply it first and go back to add in details over top. This way you won't ruin your hard work at the final stage!

FIXING MISTAKES AND OTHER TIPS AND TRICKS

Here are a few other little tips that I'd like to share before you start your neon rock-painting journey.

PATIENCE

Painted rocks can take many hours, if not days, to complete. Patience is key. If you rush, you may make mistakes that could have been avoided. That being said, don't worry too much about tiny imperfections. In the grand scheme of things, they often go unnoticed in all the other details.

HANDY HINT

Speed up drying time between coats by using a hair dryer on a low setting.

DOT FIX

Dropped an uneven dot or made one so big it ran into the others? Depending on where and when in the process this happens, you may be able to wipe the paint away using some water and a brush, or scrape the mistake off with a stick or some fine sandpaper. It is safer to allow the area (if not the entire stone) to dry before you try to fix mistakes. Clear away any flakes before repainting the area with the same colour as the underlying coat. Allow the new paint to dry and reapply your dot. It's like it never happened!

ACRYLIC 'ERASER'

The good thing about acrylic paint is that it is very thick – you can use it to paint over a mistake without the original paint showing through. The base colour is your friend! Use it as an 'eraser' for small mistakes. Don't like the dot colour you have chosen? Dot right over the top of it. Voila!

WONKY DESIGN

If you didn't quite start in the middle and your design is off centre, use more base paint to even out the circle, thus centring your design. If you have messed up more than it's worth taking the time to fix, scrub off the paint using soap and water. It is just a rock, after all!

CLEAR FINISH SPRAY

After pencilling your design onto a stone or on the base coat, spray the stone with a coat of clear finish and allow it to dry before beginning to paint. This prevents the pencil marks or base paint from mixing into the paint of the design, especially when many brush strokes are involved.

Before You Begin

Here are a few tips before you start your rock-painting journey.

Plan Ahead

Sketch out your design idea before you start. Trace the shape of your stone onto a piece of paper so you can get an idea what will fit on your 'canvas'. Use a ruler and drawing compass to practise making circles and other geometric shapes. It is helpful to get the hang of a pattern on paper before it's set on stone.

Dot Practice

Practise, practise, practise! Precision with dots takes a steady hand and knowing how place the brush or stick with just the right pressure. Dip your tool into the paint often to leave a thick, nicely saturated dot. This means that your dot is less likely to need a second coat of paint, and you are less likely to make a mistake. Try out different styles of dot art and practise making shapes and patterns. Before starting, use the dotting tool to do a test dot on some paper to get a feel for how the paint will transfer and what pressure is needed for an evenly shaped circular dot.

Brush-Stroke Practice

Brushes come in different sizes and shapes to create different paint strokes. Use a large flat brush to cover big areas and a small, round brush for details and outlines. Paint large areas or backgrounds first. Start with mid to bright colours and then add dark colours.

Handy Hint

If you can't find the perfect stone for the design you want to paint, try forming your own 'rocks' using store-bought polymer clay.

X MARKS THE DOT

SIMPLE IN DESIGN AND A GREAT WAY TO PRACTISE DOTS, THIS PATTERN CAN BE DONE ON ANY SIZE OR SHAPE OF STONE WITH VERY ATTRACTIVE RESULTS. YOU CAN ALSO MIX IT UP BY DOING SMALL HEARTS OR TINY CROSSES INSTEAD OF DOTS FOR SOMETHING DIFFERENT.

YOU WILL NEED:

- Stone
- Pencil
- Ruler (optional)
- Dotting tool: small
- Paintbrushes: small, large
- Paint: white
- Neon paint: purple, green, yellow, orange, pink
- Protective finish

1 Use a pencil to mark where the dots will be painted on the stone. You can use a ruler or estimate where the centre will be. Begin with a dotted X in the centre of the stone. Mark the centre dot, which is larger than the other dots in the design. Form the X out from the centre dot to the edges, using smaller, evenly spaced dots. The first four dots should form a square around the centre.

2 Use a small dotting tool and neon purple paint to dot over the pencil outline. This creates an X dividing the stone into four quarters of dotted rows that will form into V-shapes or 'arrows' as you continue.

3 Pencil in the next row of dots in each of the quarters. Beginning in one of the sections, align the next dot with the purple dot in both vertical and horizontal lines. Align each new dot with the others around it using the same spacing, across the stone on all sides. Do this for each of the quarters.

4 Prime the next row of dots in white paint and allow them to dry. Use a small dotting tool and dot exactly as you want it to look when you are painting in colour. The lighter neon colours are not as opaque as regular craft paint and the dark background often shows through.

HANDY HINT

This design looks great on a light-coloured rock, or you can paint it darker to contrast with the bright neon paint. Use a large brush to cover the stone with one or two coats of black or dark-coloured paint. If your stone is dark enough already, skip the base coat and spray it with a coat of clear finish. If you do paint a base coat, evenly coat the visible area (top and sides) and allow it to dry.

5 Once the white paint has dried, use the same dotting tool to paint these arrows neon green. When you paint over the white base coat with neon, the colour will be much brighter with just one coat.

HaNDY HINT

It is important to keep turning the stone often so that you can view the design as either an X or a +. This helps with estimating where to place new dots. Think of the design as a square grid with a dot at each intersecting line.

6 Continue forming the next dotted rows using the method in steps 4 and 5 until you have three arrows in each section. The order of paint colours after the purple centre X is neon green, neon yellow and neon orange. Be sure to completely cover any visible white paint. You can add a different colour over the centre dot once it is dry to make it stand out. I used pink here.

7 In the small V spaces inside the orange arrows, form small heart shapes using a small brush and white paint.

8 Allow the white paint to dry and paint the hearts in neon pink. Allow the whole design to dry, then apply a second coat (or more) to the dots if needed. Always leave it to dry completely between coats.

9 When complete, evenly coat the rock with 1–2 coats of protective finish. Dry it between finishing coats and leave the stone to cure overnight before handling.

TRIANGLED

THIS SIMPLE GEOMETRIC DESIGN IS ALL ABOUT PERCEPTION. YOU MAY CATCH YOURSELF WONDERING IF THIS DESIGN IS MADE UP OF LINES BETWEEN TRIANGLES OR TRIANGLES BETWEEN LINES! AS YOU PAINT THIS ROCK, ALL KINDS OF SHAPES AND PATTERNS BEGIN TO EMERGE, DEPENDING ON HOW YOU LOOK AT IT.

YOU WILL NEED:

- Stone
- Painter's or masking tape
- Ruler
- Craft blade
- Cutting board
- Paintbrushes: small, large
- Paint: grey, white, blue, purple
- Neon paint: pink, yellow, green, orange
- Protective finish

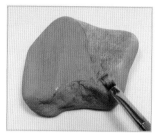

1 First, cover your rock with a grey base coat using a large round or flat brush.

2 To create thin strips of tape, layer 6–8 pieces of tape (make these strips longer than the size of your stone) one on top of another. Very carefully, use a craft blade to cut very thin strips. It helps to use a ruler to keep the blade from slipping. Cut more than you need to get the best selection. It is tricky to get such small strips all evenly sized.

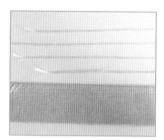

3 When you are finished, you should be able to peel the tape layers apart and have 6–8 strips of tape for each cut you make.

4 Next, lay a row of strips across the stone horizontally, parallel to one another, measuring about 1 cm (0.4 in) of space between each strip. Firmly press the edges of the strips to the stone so that little to no paint will be able to seep underneath when painted. Lay another row of parallel strips diagonally to the left over the top of the others, again with 1 cm (0.4 in) of space between them, making a diamond pattern. Lay a final row of strips, this time diagonally and to the right on top of the others. These strips should cross directly over the intersections of the other strips. Don't worry too much if your triangles are not exact in size; this can be adjusted later.

5 Ensure all tape is securely fixed to the stone, paying close attention to the intersecting areas or any areas where there are small indents, cracks or holes. Use a larger brush or a sponge to cover the top of the stone in white paint as a primer, painting over the tape. Allow to dry and apply a second coat if needed.

6 When the white paint is completely dry, use whatever colours you like to paint the triangles. You can use all neon colours or a mix of neon and regular paints.

7 Now comes the fun part! Carefully peel off the tape to reveal the design. Go strip by strip, removing the top layer first. Peel slowly: you don't want to peel up any paint that should remain stuck with the stone. Voila!

8 Because of a stone's uneven surface, it is likely you will have to fix up the outlines by going over any uneven lines with the stone colour or filling in triangles with the appropriate colour of paint. Use a small detail or liner brush. When complete, evenly coat the rock with 1–2 coats of protective finish.

HANDY HINT

The potential colour combinations are endless: try a mix of both neon and regular colours, or just two or three neon colours throughout.

SPIKED STONE

YOU KNOW THAT HARDENED ACRYLIC PAINT THAT HAS SAT OUT A BIT TOO LONG OR THE CHUNKS OF PAINT YOU FIND ON YOUR LIDS? YOU COULD CONSIDER IT A WASTE, ONLY FIT FOR THE TRASH, OR YOU COULD USE IT TO TURN YOUR ROCKS INTO THESE SPIKED LITTLE CURIOSITIES!

YOU WILL NEED:

- Stone
- Dotting tools: small, medium, large
- Paintbrushes: medium, large
- Paint: black or navy, white
- Neon paint: pink, green, orange, yellow
- Protective finish

1. Paint a base coat. With a large round or flat brush, paint all visible parts of the stone using a dark shade of navy blue or black paint. Allow to dry and apply a second coat if needed. Allow to dry completely before moving on.

HANDY HINT

If you have a metallic paint colour, try adding a few drops of silver to the navy or black base for a little shimmer!

2. Use white paint to dot the design on the stone. This priming step may seem tedious, but it saves time and paint if you're using bright neon colours over a dark base. Start with the strip of dots down the centre. Use a medium-sized dotting tool or round brush to place the largest dot at the centre of the stone (5 mm, 0.2 in). Continue dotting to the edge with slightly tapered dots that get smaller as they reach the ends. On either side of the centre dotted line, add a line of small, close (without touching) dots from end to end. Allow all dots to dry.

3. On either side of the centre lines, use a large dotting tool to place another large dot half way along the row of dots. Continue the row with large dots getting smaller towards each edge, keeping some space between them. Add a ring of tiny dots around each large dot. Space permitting, add another tapered row of large dots, circling each dot with a ring of tiny dots.

HANDY HINT

The process of tapering dots is used in some of the different activities in this book. Keep this term in mind as you'll see it again later!

4. Use a small dotting tool to add dots in the remaining space on either side of the original centre lines and around the larger ringed dots. Keep them small and spaced apart. If your paint is opaque enough, do these small dots with neon pink paint. If not, fill the space with white dots.

5 If you painted with white for the small dots in step 4, paint over the white with neon pink. Leave the dotted rings around the large dots as white, and also leave the small dotted lines that are on either side of the centre line as white.

HaNDY HINT

If your paint is not thick, you can thicken acrylic paint by leaving it exposed to air; allow some of the moisture to evaporate, but not so much that it dries out completely. Often artist or premium-brand acrylic paint is thicker than craft paint, or you can check under the lids of your paints for paint that has started to dry and is thicker than the rest. You can also use paints called 3-dimensional or puff paint for raised dots, which are sold in craft stores.

6 Paint the centre row of dots neon green, leaving the small dots on either side white. Paint the next row of large dots on either side neon orange. Leave the ring of small dots white. Paint the last rows of large dots closest to the edges neon green. Start spiking the green and orange dots using thick paint. Saturate your small dotting tool well then dab it to the stone. Pull it up and off quickly, so the paint is pulled upwards and stays raised. Do this a few times until a little spike forms. If your paint is thick enough to form a peak, then one or two coats should be enough. You do not need to allow the paint to dry completely, as having the paint not quite dry is helpful to the spiking process. When done, allow all paint to dry. Generally, the spikes will dry as you have left them but if they have receded while drying, apply another coat in the same manner and allow to dry again.

7 Top off all the green and orange spikes with a light dab of neon yellow. Be careful to dab lightly so as not to damage the spikes. While they are dry to touch, they are not yet cured and could potentially get knocked down. If the yellow does not appear very bright over the green and orange, prime the tips with white paint and allow to dry before painting over with yellow. Allow everything to dry for at least 1–2 hours.

8 Apply 1–2 coats of finish and allow to dry for at least 24 hours to ensure the peaks stay strong. Once cured, the paint spikes are actually quite flexible and should bend and retain their form if pressed on.

sea urcHin

For this fun dot design reminiscent of those little ocean creatures, use neon paint to highlight regular paint colours. Choosing a circular stone adds to the symmetry of the design and mimics a sea-urchin shape; however, you can paint the design on just about any stone with enough flattened areas.

YOU WILL NEED:

- Stone
- Drawing compass (optional)
- Dotting tools: small, medium, large
- Paintbrushes: small, medium, large
- Paint: black, pink, yellow, bright blue or turquoise, yellow-orange, aqua, purple, light purple, light orange, mid-orange, dark orange, dark purple, red-orange, red
- Neon paint: yellow, orange, pink, green
- Protective finish

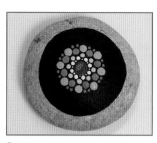

1 Use a drawing compass or sketch a base circle to cover most of the stone, leaving the edges exposed. With a larger round brush, fill in the circle with black paint. Allow to dry and, using pink paint and your dotting tool, place a dot in the centre. Generally, regular craft paint is opaque enough that you can use one or two coats and not need to prime before using bright colours.

2 Using a smaller tool, place eight small white dots evenly around the centre dot. Keep all dots apart from each other. In the small spaces between these white dots, closer to the pink dot, use your tool and a steady hand to place eight extra tiny dots. Continue on to the next ring of small dots, keeping them the same size as the white but using bright yellow paint. These dots are staggered, placed just below the spaces between the small white dots.

3 Paint a ring of staggered, slightly larger dots. Use bright blue or turquoise paint. Add the next ring of staggered dots using yellow-orange. Make these dots slightly larger again: 3–4 mm in diameter. These are slightly sunk into the spaces between the bright blue, without touching each other. In the space between the yellow-orange dots, just below the bright blue dots, place two small aqua dots side by side.

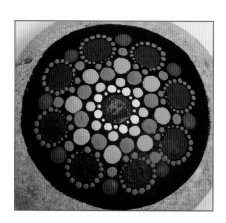

4 Directly below and aligned between these aqua dots, use a small brush or large dotting tool for purple-coloured dots about 5 mm (0.2 in) in diameter. Space them out and add a ring of tiny light purple dots around each one. Make the dots in the ring taper down in size as you reach the aqua dots. In the space between the ringed purple dots, place a small light orange dot. Directly below, add another slightly larger mid-orange dot.

5 Between the orange dots and in line with the ringed purple dots, use a small brush and a deeper shade of purple to form slightly larger dots, leaving some space around them. Use your large dotting tool and dark orange paint to place dots about 5 mm (0.2 in) in between the dark purple dots. Use a small dotting tool to complete two tapered tiny dotted rings in white around the purple dots. End the second outermost white ring as you reach the dark orange dots.

6 Finish the rows of orange dots with a red-orange and a red dot, using whatever size will fit. Allow all paint to dry to touch for 15 minutes or so. All yellow, orange and red dots should be in a relatively straight line out from the centre, and all blue and purple dots should be in a straight line from the centre.

7 Use neon colours to add dots. Using the appropriately sized dotting tool, place a smaller dot on each of the dots, apart from the tiny rings and white dots. Put neon yellow on yellow dots, neon orange on orange, neon pink on red and in the centre icon, and neon green on the blue. Place neon pink on the purple dots and for the largest purple dots, use a dot of non-neon lighter purple; once this has dried, add a tiny dot of neon pink.

8 Allow all paint to dry and apply 1–2 coats of protective finish before leaving to set for 24 hours.

INFINITY STONE

Behold your very own hand-held galaxy! This design is amazingly simple. You won't need any special tools to form this swirling design. Once you start the pattern, you will see the spiral naturally emerge from the placement of dots that increase in size with each new ring. Adding colour sends you spiralling off into infinity!

YOU WILL NEED:

- Stone
- Dotting tools: small, medium, large
- Paintbrushes: large
- Paint: black, white, light blue, mid-blue, dark blue
- Neon paint: purple, pink, yellow, blue
- Protective finish

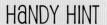

1 Use a relatively flat stone so that you have space to expand out the spiral formation. A round shape is not necessary but does add to the symmetry of the design. Choose a stone that is at least 5 cm (2 in) across, as you will need room on the stone for the centre dot and spiral. Use a large brush and paint over the whole stone using a black base colour. Allow to dry.

2 Prime the dot design using white paint and your dotting tool of choice. Place a dot of about 8 mm (0.3 in) in diameter in the centre of the stone. This dot needs to be large enough to fit 24 tiny dots, evenly spaced around it without touching.

3 Once you have your centre icon surrounded by 24 evenly spaced, tiny dots, the rest of the design is fairly easy. Begin the next ring of dots, staggered so that they are above the spaces between the previous dots of the ring. Make them slightly larger than the last ring. Do not sink them into the space: just align them as a new ring.

HANDY HINT

Practise this dot design on paper beforehand so you get the hang of how it works. Experiment with using different colours if you wish.

HANDY HINT

The number of dots is important as it determines the number of colours you can use for the swirls. Having an even number allows for equal colour distribution. With 24, there are six sections, each with four different colours: one shade of purple followed by three shades of blue.

4 Continue adding rings of dots, making each one larger than the previous ring. Don't rush! Alignment, as well as gradually increasing in dot size with each new ring, is key to making this design. It is important to turn the stone as you dot to get the best dot alignment possible.

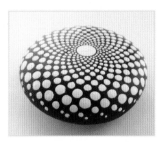
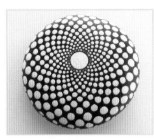

5 Continue adding rings of dots until you have covered the stone to the edge, spilling over the side if possible. Finish the design by tapering the dots down in size for the last few rings that reach over the sides and under the stone. Allow all dots to dry, then hold the stone away from you to get a different perspective. This view allows you to see if any dots could use a touch-up so they're a bit larger or smaller, or if they need adjusting to be better aligned.

6 Paint with colour. Use three shades of blue (light blue, mid-blue, dark blue) and bright neon purple. Whatever colours you use, keep them in the same order from start to finish. Start by painting the smallest dots around the centre icon. Begin with purple, followed by light blue, mid-blue and dark blue in that order. Repeat the colour pattern until the ring is complete.

7 For the next ring, move the colour pattern one dot over, going in a counter-clockwise direction. Beginning again with purple, place the dot above and to the right of the same colour dot in the ring before it. Continue to paint the colours in the same order, changing colour dot by dot for at least the first 3–4 rings, until you can clearly see where each colour is curving away from the centre.

8 Now you can save time by finishing each colour one at a time, row by row (i.e. all purple dots, then all light blue, and so on), rather than alternating colours dot by dot, one ring at a time. Allow all paint to dry and apply the second coating if needed.

9 Paint the centre icon dark blue. Go over the blue and purple dots with a slightly lighter colour. Add a tiny dot of neon pink on the purple, neon blue on the mid-blue, mid-blue on the dark blue, and finally a very light blue on the light blue.

10 To finish, add some bright stars to this galaxy. Use your small dotting tool to make tiny neon yellow dots in all the little spaces around each dot. Do this as far up from the sides toward the centre as you can fit, without touching other dots. Add a smaller dot of mid-blue to the centre dot and top it with a tiny dot of light blue, allowing each to dry between coats.

11 Do any touch-ups or second coatings and when all paint is dry, apply one or two coats of protective finish and leave to dry for 24 hours.

OWL FRIEND

TIRED OF DOTTING? PAINT A NEW OWL FRIEND! HE LOOKS LIKE HE MAY SUFFER FROM IRRITABLE OWL SYNDROME, BUT DON'T LET HIS SCOWL RUFFLE YOUR FEATHERS: HE'S A HOOT AND A SOLID FRIEND FOR SURE! OWL TRY TO KEEP THE PUNS TO A MINIMUM...

YOU WILL NEED:

Stone

Pencil

Paintbrushes: small, large

Thin brush or black paint pen

Paint: white, orange, black

Neon paint: orange, yellow, pink, blue, green, purple

Protective finish

HANDY HINT

Before beginning, draw or trace the outline of your stone on paper and practise your owl-making skills. Different-shaped stones may require small adjustments, but generally this design can work on just about any size or shape of stone, provided you have room for the eyes and wings. I have used a flattened egg-shaped stone with the larger end for the head and the narrower end for the body and wing area.

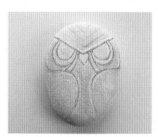

1 Use a large brush to prime your stone with 1–2 coats of white paint. Allow to dry. Lightly pencil the main outline of the owl on the stone. Draw the brow as a V shape about a third of the way down. Add the beak as a smaller V connected to the point of the brow. Lightly pencil in the eyes as partial circles connected to the brow on each side of the beak. Make sure they are the same size and evenly spaced. Draw the remaining V lines in the brow and continue forming the eyes. Shape another ring around the pupil and begin a third ring, but leave this unfinished, stopping just below the beak. Draw the wings coming inwards from the edges of the stone to just before the centre, curving downwards and ending at the bottom. Finish drawing in the third eye circles, continuing the curved line from the brow on either side of the beak to the wing. At the edge of the stone, continue the curve of the line from the wing to the line. Add parallel lines connecting the middle eye circles closest to the beak.

2 Go over your outline for symmetry and adjust your lines with pencil and/or white paint if necessary. Adjust the outline using pencil and/or white paint as necessary. Once you have the outline of the owl's main features, begin painting. Paint the front area between the wings with orange paint, allow to dry, then add a coat of neon orange over top. This will darken the neon shade and make the other colours nearby appear brighter in contrast. Inside the iris circle, lightly pencil in the pupil. Leave a 5 mm (0.2 in) tapered space for the iris. Use a small round brush to paint the iris neon yellow, allow to dry, then paint in the pupil with black paint. Let all paint dry, during which time you can lightly pencil in 5–6 lines spanning off the second eye circle, crossing through the rings to the wing and outer edges of the stone.

3 Use a thin brush or paint pen to go over any pencil outlines. Use white paint to even out lines and fix any mistakes. Dry for 20 minutes or more; you want to be sure the black and white paint are dry before painting over the top.

4 Paint the brow's V lines: paint the largest neon pink, followed by neon yellow, then neon blue. Allow to dry. Use a pencil to lightly outline the detail of the wings. Draw a straight horizontal line across the top third of each wing. Below this, draw four or five vertical lines to form thick stripes. Use a small detail brush and begin to outline the top portion of the wing in black paint; trace alongside the inner top wing shape to leave a thin white border space between the shape (painted in purple with black outline) and the edge of the wing. While this is drying, paint the beak neon orange. While this dries, outline the lower portion of the wing with black and, when dry, use neon green and neon yellow paint for the stripes.

5 While this dries, paint the little sections within the eye area. Beginning closest to the beak moving outwards, paint the sections in the first ring neon orange, pink and purple. Paint the next ring neon green, neon blue and neon orange. The outer spaces to the side of the stone are painted neon green, blue, pink and yellow.

6 Allow all paint to dry before adding a second coat or touch-up if needed. When the paint has completely dried (30–60 mins or more), use a small round brush and white paint to add the front diamond shapes and dots in the brow as well as across the purple part of the wings. In the blue top part of the brow, add another small V that extends over the edge of the stone into a heart shape. Apart from the dots, outline all the new white details in black once they are dry.

7 In the lower portion of the wings, add in a thin black chevron detail within the green stripes. When the white paint is dry, carefully paint the wing dots neon pink, the front diamonds neon yellow, the brow dots neon purple in the yellow section, neon green in the blue section and use neon orange for the top brow heart that falls over the edge. Finally add a little white gleam in the black of the owl's eyes. Leave for 2–3 hours or more to ensure the paint is well set and dry.

8 Apply 1–2 coats of protective finish and leave to cure for 24 hours.

New Bass Friend

Coral reefs are among the most colourful and biodiverse environments on the planet. Bring a bit of that underwater wonder to dry land with this bright little fish friend. Remember, you can swap around any colours you like to make a wonderfully colourful fish family!

YOU WILL NEED:

- Stone
- Pencil and paper
- Dotting tools: small, medium, large
- Paintbrushes: small, large
- Thin brush or black paint pen
- Paint: white, black
- Neon paint: pink, yellow, purple, orange, blue, green
- Protective finish

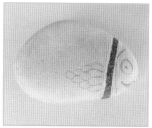

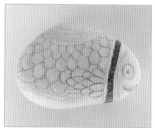

1 Use a brush to paint the top and sides of the stone with a base coat of white paint. Leave a line of space between the head and body free of paint, allowing the stone to peek through as an added detail. The head should cover about a quarter of the stone. Let the paint fully dry, then lightly pencil in a line running along inside the gap in the paint, dividing the head and body. Pencil in the eye and mouth, and a curved line for a gill. Lightly draw in the lower side fin along the unpainted line in the bottom half of the stone using small bumps or C shapes. Start with the greatest number of these shapes along the unpainted line, and continue the next row in a scalloped fish-scale formation, beginning and ending on the centre tip of the scale before it. Each row of scales decreases in number by one, ending at the tip with a single scale. The number of scales you begin with will vary depending on the size of the stone and how wide you draw them. This stone's fin started with four scales along the head line.

2 Starting at the top of the body area, pencil three curved lines on top of each other, covering no more than the top quarter of the stone. The last and longest curved line is the baseline along which you will make the first row of scales. Draw in U-shaped bumps or scales running the full length under the lowest curved line. Form the next row of scales below the first in a scalloped pattern. Unlike the vertically scalloped fin scales, these rows go horizontally across the body. To make these rows work around the fin and the head section, start new rows at these places and continue the row to the other end of the stone. Make the final new row when you are about three-quarters of the way down the stone, then add two parallel lines loosely following the line of the scales underneath them.

3 Paint in the colours, beginning with the head. Use a small round brush and paint the head neon pink. Paint the eye and mouth with white paint and neon yellow outlining the gill. Outline all of these head features with black paint or an extra-fine paint pen and add the pupil in the eye. Allow to dry, moving on to the body area. Go over all the pencil outlines with an extra-small detail brush and black paint. Use white paint to even out lines or fix mistakes. While the black outline dries, paint the large area at the bottom and the top half-circle with neon purple paint. Outline the purple areas in black. Once the black outline is dry, paint the second half-circle at the top in neon pink, followed by white in the next half-circle.

4 Paint the body scales using a small round pointed brush to get in the corners. Paint in rows, starting from top to bottom, completing the side fin scales last. Allow the paint to fully dry before applying more coats. The first row of body scales is neon yellow, after which the neon colours are pink, orange, blue and green. After the green scales, leave some white space between the scales and the purple bottom. Use neon paint on the side fin, starting with blue then orange, pink and yellow for the tip. Add a thin neon pink line running above the black border on the purple underside.

5 Add neon yellow dot detailing to the area of exposed stone; white and neon pink dots in the purple area below the bottom line; a few white dots around the eye; and neon blue dots in the white above the bottom line. Allow all paint to dry before adding a second coat if needed. When the paint has dried completely, go over the outline using an extra-small round-tipped detail brush and black paint where needed. Add in the scale details with black: a curved line inside each of the body scales and little sprout lines ending in a dot inside all scales, including the fin scales. Add in two green dots and a pink dot at the base of the blue fin scales where they meet the head and body line.

6 Add more dots to the top half-circles: white paint in the pink and neon green in the purple. Add a row of neon yellow dots under the rows of white and pink dots in the bottom purple section. Dot in a tiny white dot in the sprout shapes on all of the body fins. When all is dry, apply one or two coats of protective finish and leave to dry and fully harden for 24 hours.

HANDY HINT

If you want to paint the fish on both sides of the stone, do the steps one side at a time so that you are not flipping back and forth, which can lead to problems, especially during painting. Protect the completed side from scratches or paint splatters with a piece of plastic wrap or painter's tape while you mirror the design on the other side.

HANDY HINT

Painting a black outline of equal thickness as well as small details can be challenging. I recommend getting a good liner/detail brush. Using an extra-fine-tipped paint pen or permanent marker can do the trick but you can achieve more delicate lines when using paint and a brush.

rock Garden

'IF I HaD a FLOWer FOR every TIMe I THOUGHT OF YOU, I COULD WALK THROUGH MY GARDEN FOREVER.'
MAKE a FLOWER FOR YOUR FOREVER GARDEN. THESE PRETTY POSIES ARE JUST THE PERFECT FLOWER: THEY STAY
IN BLOOM ALL YEAR, NEED NO CARE AND NEVER WILT! THIS CONCENTRIC DESIGN CAN BE CREATED USING AS MANY
DIFFERENT COLOURS AND DETAILS AS YOU CAN IMAGINE.

YOU WILL NEED:

- Stone
- Pencil
- Dotting tools: small, medium, large
- Paintbrushes: small, large
- Thin brush or white and black paint pens (both optional)
- Paint: white, black, red, light pink
- Neon paint: pink, yellow
- Protective finish

1 Use a large round brush to paint a white circle or oval on top of the stone. Leave some space around the edges. When the paint has dried, lightly pencil a flower. Begin the outline in the centre of the stone. Pencil in a small dot and add larger circles around it. From this circle, there will be many thin lines spanning out around it, but don't draw them yet. Rather, where the lines will end, lightly pencil in another circle. Begin to form the first petals – small rounded bumps all the way around the circle, like a cloud shape.

2 Begin painting the flower. Fill in the cloud shape with a small round brush and black paint. Allow the black paint to dry completely and apply a second coat if needed. Pencil in another ring of larger bumpy petals, about twice the size of the previous ones. Stagger these petals in relation to the last by starting and finishing each new petal bump at the top and centre of the black bumps beneath. Finish the flower outline by using white paint and adding a third ring of staggered bumpy petals along the outer edges of the oval base. Make them larger than those before it.

3 Use a small round detail brush or extra-fine-tip paint pen to outline the remainder of the flower petals in black. Leave a thin outline of white around the entire flower.

4 In the middle of the black petal area, use a small round brush and red paint to form a circle in the centre of the flower. Let the red paint dry completely then use a dotting tool to place a dot in the centre with black paint. Make this small enough to leave the edge of the red exposed, but large enough to fit another dot inside it. When the black paint has dried, add a white dot just large enough that the black slightly shows as an outline around it. Dot a small ring inside the red circle with white paint.

HANDY HINT

Brush strokes tend to thin out the neon paint, making it more translucent and leading to streaks. Apply thin coats and let them dry completely before applying a new coat. If it is a small area, try dabbing paint on instead of using brush strokes.

5 Use a thin detail brush and white paint or an extra-fine white paint pen to add lots of thin white lines extending out from the red circle to where the black petals begin. Do this all the way around, placing a tiny white dot on the end of each thin line. Use black paint to thin out and neaten any white lines as well as outline around the red circle.

6 Paint in all the petals with a small brush and neon pink paint, leaving a small space of white outline between the pink paint and the petals of the ring before. Once the pink paint has dried, use white paint (pen or brush) over the top of any pink to create a nice even outline around each petal. Allow all paint to dry. Apply more coats if needed, drying completely between each coat. With a small round brush, add stripes to the outer ring of petals with light pink paint (not neon). Once all paint has completely dried, go over the outlines with black and white paint to make them sharper and cleaner. Use an extra-small round detail brush or paint pen to clean up the outlines within the design, including the centre dot, the red dot and each black petal outline. Clean up the white outline around the petals and the entire flower.

7 Add in the petal detailing. In the second ring of petals, form a thin curved black line inside each petal over the pink paint Add another coat of neon pink in the border formed by the black line. Then add a little black sprout ending in a dot in the middle of each petal, and use a small dotting tool to add a neon yellow dot in the centre of each one, leaving a black outline. In the outer ring of petals, thinly outline each stripe. Allow all paint to dry and go over any mistakes using the colour of paint you use as an 'eraser.'

8 When all paint is dry, spray with 1–2 coats of finishing spray and leave it to dry overnight.

congratulations!

You have made some beautifully bright rocks of art. Whether they're cute critters or astounding patterns, there's lots of ways you can decorate and delight with your creations! Keep them as a treat for yourself or give them as gifts; put them in a houseplant or brighten up your garden; place them on a shelf or in a little treasure box; pop them in an aquarium or keep them as your own pet rock... They are sure to bring a bright, colourful piece of happiness wherever they are!

What will you do next? You could take your art to the internet! Connect with other artists who love to paint amazing rock designs, and get inspired with new ideas of your own. Take pictures of your stones in various settings, and make a social media page so you can show off your art.

Get inspired and continue your rock-painting journey! Neon colours are bright, bold and energetic, and, most of all, fun!

always remember to think happy dots!

a note on the author

Hi! My name is Katie Cameron and I live in beautiful Halifax, Nova Scotia. I am a postal worker by night and, more recently, rock artist by day. I have no prior art experience but I have always loved colourful patterns and been fascinated by rocks and minerals. It was in my search of these where I first encountered the works of other great 'dotillists' and knew I had to try making my own painted rocks. It was no time at all before I was hooked on making dots! I created HFXrocks to share these little treasures with the world and have been dotting along ever since.